Kitten

Jinny Johnson

W
FRANKLIN WATTS
LONDON•SYDNEY

An Appleseed Editions book

First published in 2013 by Franklin Watts
338 Euston Road, London NW1 3BH

Franklin Watts Australia
Hachette Children's Books
Level 17/207 Kent St, Sydney, NSW 2000

© 2013 Appleseed Editions

Created by Appleseed Editions Ltd,
Well House, Friars Hill, Guestling,
East Sussex TN35 4ET

Designed by Guy Callaby
Edited by Mary-Jane Wilkins
Illustrations by Bill Donohoe

ISBN 978 1 4451 2197 0

Dewey Classification 636.8'07

A CIP record for this book is available from
the British Library.

Photo acknowledgements
l = left, r = right, t = top, b = bottom
title page Smit; 2 OKSun; 3t Terrie L. Zeller
b Volodymyr Krasyuk; 4 Reddogs; 7 Senchilin;
11 Catherine Murray; 12 Magone; 15 Komar;
16 bonchan; 19 Ewa Studio; 23 forestpath.
Front cover Inha Makeyeva
All images Shutterstock

Printed in China

Franklin Watts is a division of Hachette Children's Books,
an Hachette company.
www.hachette.co.uk

Contents

I'm very excited. My mum says we can have a kitten.

I want to know all about cats and kittens so I can look after my pet well.

Here's what I have found out.

Pet **cats** belong to the same group of animals as lions and tigers.

Cats can live for 16 years or more, so we will have our pet for a long time.

Cats make **great** family pets. They are good company, clean and lots of fun.

They do need careful looking after, and plenty of **attention**, especially during the first few months.

There are lots of different kinds of cats to choose from.

Cats may be black, white, black and white, brown, grey or ginger. Tabbies have stripy markings.

A cat meows for attention. It might want food, or just a stroke and a cuddle.

There are also **pedigree** cats, such as Persians, Siamese and Burmese. Some have long hair and can be hard to look after.

Kittens need to stay with their mum until they are about eight weeks old.

We will choose a kitten with bright eyes, a clean nose and shiny fur. We will check that it moves well and breathes quietly. A **healthy** kitten shouldn't sneeze or snuffle.

Cats can run fast and jump up high. They have very good senses of smell, hearing, sight and touch.

Before we get my kitten,
my dad and I will make sure
we have everything it needs.

We will buy some **food** and
water bowls,
and maybe
a few **toys**.

*We'll buy a cat carrier
for our kitten to travel in.*

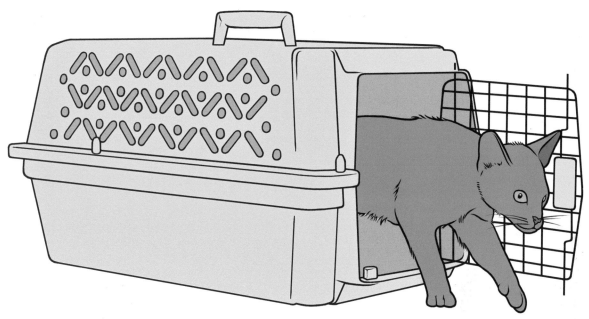

My kitten must stay in
for the first few weeks
so it will need a **litter tray**.

All cats are **meat-eaters**. They can't live on vegetables.

A kitten aged between eight and twelve weeks needs **four** or **five** small meals a day.

By the age of six months, a young cat needs just **two** meals a day.

Try to find out what your kitten has been eating so you can give it the same food until it is used to its new home.

13

We will buy **canned** and **packet** foods for my kitten. Cats can also eat **dry** food.

People think cats need milk. Some enjoy milk, but it isn't good for them.

We'll see which food my kitten likes best.

We can also cook **fresh** food such as chicken and fish sometimes.

I will always make sure my kitten has fresh, clean **water** to drink.

Cats and kittens like plenty of **sleep**. I will let my kitten sleep and not disturb it.

Cats keep themselves clean but they like to be brushed. Brushing helps to get rid of loose hair.

A cat **grooms** itself every day. It licks a paw and wipes it over its face, then cleans its front legs, back legs, tummy and tail.

A cat's **bendy** body lets it twist and turn to reach almost every part.

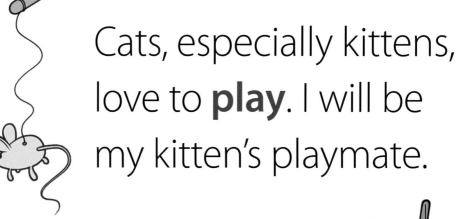

Cats, especially kittens, love to **play**. I will be my kitten's playmate.

My mum is going to help me make holes in a box so my kitten can have fun running in and out.

I'll find some **cotton reels** and **ping-pong balls** for my kitten, and we might buy a **toy mouse**, too.

I will make sure the toys are safe for my kitten. I won't let it play with anything sharp or breakable.

Hooray! I have my new kitten. He is a boy and he's eight weeks old.

I'm letting my kitten get used to me before I try to pick him up and cuddle him. I speak **softly** to my kitten and stroke him gently.

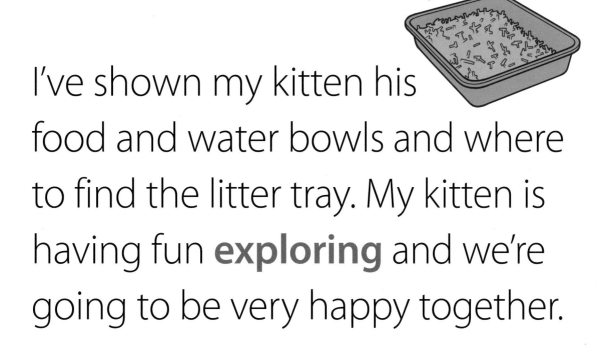

I've shown my kitten his food and water bowls and where to find the litter tray. My kitten is having fun **exploring** and we're going to be very happy together.

Notes for parents

Choosing a pet
Make sure you choose a healthy kitten. Try to find a kitten raised in a family home, as it will be used to children. You might also try your local animal shelter, but explain you want a family pet and ask their advice. Wherever you find your kitten, take it to the vet for a health check and advice on vaccinations.

First days
Keep your kitten indoors until it is used to its new home. It shouldn't go outside until it has been vaccinated.

Health
Make sure your pet is looked after properly. Supervise feeding and show your child how to pick up and hold the kitten. Neuter your pet cat to reduce the number of unwanted animals. Ask your vet for advice on this. You might want to have your pet microchipped in case it gets lost. A chip with a unique number is injected into the skin at the back of its neck. This doesn't hurt. The number can be read by a scanner if necessary.

Words to remember

pedigree
A pedigree animal is a particular breed, such as a Siamese or a Persian. It usually has a certificate with details of its parents.

groom
To care for and clean the fur. Cats groom themselves by licking their fur. Brush and comb your cat to help it stay clean.

vaccination
An injection given by the vet to prevent your kitten catching serious illnesses.

Index